PRAYERS
Written At Vailima

by

Robert Louis Stevenson

Introduction by Mrs. R. L. Stevenson

Catherine Kanner
Artist

Penelope Glass
Editor

CALAMUS
Los Angeles, California
2000

For Charles Kanner

IN EVERY SAMOAN household the day is closed with prayer and the singing of hymns. The omission of this sacred duty would indicate not only a lack of religious training in the house chief, but a shameless disregard of all that is reputable in Samoan social life. No doubt, to many, the evening service is no more than a duty fulfilled. The child who says his prayer at his mother's knee can have no real conception of the meaning of the words he lisps so readily, yet he goes to his little bed with a sense of heavenly protection that he would miss were the prayer forgotten. The average Samoan is but a larger child in most things, and would lay an uneasy head on his wooden pillow if he had not joined, even perfunctorily, in the evening service. With my husband, prayer, the direct appeal, was a necessity. When he was happy he felt

impelled to offer thanks for that undeserved joy; when in sorrow, or pain, to call for strength to bear what must be borne.

Vailima lay up some three miles of continual rise from Apia, and more than half that distance from the nearest village. It was a long way for a tired man to walk down every evening with the sole purpose of joining in family worship; and the road through the bush was dark, and, to the Samoan imagination, beset with supernatural terrors. Wherefore, as soon as our household had fallen into a regular routine, and the bonds of Samoan family life began to draw us more closely together, Tusitala [Samoan for storyteller, referring to R.L.S.] felt the necessity of including our retainers in our evening devotions. I suppose ours was the only white man's family in all

Samoa, except those of the missionaries, where the day naturally ended with this homely, patriarchal custom. Not only were the religious scruples of the natives satisfied, but what we did not foresee, our own respectability—and incidentally that of our retainers—became assured, and the influence of Tusitala increased tenfold.

After all work and meals were finished, the "pu," or war conch, was sounded from the back veranda and the front, so that it might be heard by all. I don't think it ever occurred to us that there was any incongruity in the use of the war conch for the peaceful invitation to prayer. In response to its summons the white members of the family took their usual places, in one end of the large hall, while the Samoans—men, women and children—trooped in through all

the open doors, some carrying lanterns if the evening were dark, all moving quietly and dropping with Samoan decorum in a wide semicircle on the floor beneath a great lamp that hung from the ceiling. The service began by my son reading a chapter from the Samoan Bible, Tusitala following with a prayer in English, sometimes impromptu, but more often from the notes in this little book, interpolating, or changing with the circumstances of the day. Then came the singing of one or more hymns in the native tongue, and the recitation in concert of the Lord's Prayer, also in Samoan. Many of these hymns were set to ancient tunes very wild and warlike and strangely at variance with the missionary words.

Sometimes a passing band of hostile warriors, with blackened faces, would peer in at us through

the open windows, and often we were forced to
pause until the strangely savage, monotonous noise
of the native drums had ceased; but no Samoan, nor,
I trust, white person, changed his reverent attitude.
Once, I remember a look of surprised dismay
crossing the countenance of Tusitala when my son,
contrary to his usual custom of reading the next
chapter following that of yesterday, turned back the
leaves of his Bible to find a chapter fiercely
denunciatory, and only too applicable to the foreign
dictators of distracted Samoa. On another occasion
the chief, himself, brought the service to a sudden
check. He had just learned of the treacherous
conduct of one in whom he had every reason to
trust. That evening the prayer seemed unusually
short and formal. As the singing stopped he arose

abruptly and left the room. I hastened after him, fearing some sudden illness. "What is it?" I asked. "It is this" was the reply; "I am not yet fit to say 'Forgive us our trespasses as we forgive those who trespass against us.' "

It is with natural reluctance that I touch upon the last prayer of my husband's life. Many have supposed that he showed, in the wording of this prayer, that he had some premonition of his approaching death. I am sure he had no such premonition. It was I who told the assembled family that I felt an impending disaster approaching nearer and nearer. Any Scot will understand that my statement was received seriously. It could not be, we thought, that danger threatened anyone within the house; but Mr. Graham Balfour, my husband's

cousin, very near and dear to us, was away on a perilous cruise. Our fears followed the various vessels, more or less unseaworthy, in which he was making his way from island to island to the atoll where the exiled king, Mataafa, was at that time imprisoned. In my husband's last prayer, the night before his death, he asked that we should be given strength to bear the loss of this dear friend, should such a sorrow befall us.

MRS. R. L. STEVENSON

FOR SUCCESS

Lord, behold our family here assembled. We thank Thee for this place in which we dwell; for the love that unites us; for the peace accorded us this day; for the hope with which we expect the morrow; for the health, the work, the food, and the bright skies, that make our lives delightful; for our friends in all parts of the earth, and our friendly helpers in this foreign isle. Let peace abound in our small company. Purge out of every heart the lurking grudge. Give us grace and strength to forbear and to persevere. Offenders, give us the grace to accept and to forgive offenders. Forgetful ourselves, help us to bear cheerfully the forgetfulness of others. Give us courage and gaiety and the quiet mind. Spare to us our friends, soften to us our enemies. Bless us, if it may be, in all our innocent endeavors. If it may not, give us the strength to encounter that which is to come, that we be brave in peril, constant in tribulation, temperate in wrath, and in all changes of fortune, and down to the gates of death, loyal and loving one to another.

As the clay to the potter, as the windmill to the wind,
as children of their sire, we beseech of Thee this
help and mercy for Christ's sake.

FOR GRACE

Grant that we here before Thee may be set
free from the fear of vicissitude and the fear of death,
may finish what remains before us of
our course without dishonour to ourselves or hurt to
others, and, when the day comes, may die in peace.
Deliver us from fear and favor: from mean hopes
and cheap pleasures. Have mercy on each in his
deficiency; let him be not cast down; support the
stumbling on the way, and give at
last rest to the weary.

AT MORNING

The day returns and brings us the petty round
of irritating concerns and duties. Help us to play the
man, help us to perform them with laughter and
kind faces, let cheerfulness abound with industry.
Give us to go blithely on our business all this day,
bring us to our resting beds weary and content and
undishonoured, and grant us in
the end the gift of sleep.

EVENING

We come before Thee, O Lord, in the end of
thy day with thanksgiving.

   Our beloved in the far parts of the earth, those
who are now beginning the labours of the day what
time we end them, and those with whom the sun
now stands at the point of noon, bless, help,
console, and prosper them.

   Our guard is relieved, the service of the day
is over, and the hour come to rest. We resign into
thy hands our sleeping bodies, our cold hearths and
open doors. Give us to awake with smiles, give us to
labour smiling. As the sun returns in the east, so let
our patience be renewed with dawn; as the sun
lightens the world, so let our loving- kindness make
bright this house of our habitation.

ANOTHER FOR EVENING

Lord, receive our supplications for this house, family, and country. Protect the innocent, restrain the greedy and the treacherous, lead us out of our tribulation into a quiet land.

Look down upon ourselves and upon our absent dear ones. Help us and them; prolong our days in peace and honour. Give us health, food, bright weather, and light hearts. In what we mediate of evil, frustrate our will; in what of good, further our endeavors. Cause injuries to be forgot and benefits to be remembered.

Let us lie down without fear and awake and arise with exultation. For his sake, in whose words we now conclude.

IN TIME OF RAIN

We thank Thee, Lord, for the glory of the late days
and the excellent face of thy sun. We thank Thee for
good news received. We thank Thee for the
pleasures we have enjoyed and for those we have
been able to confer. And now, when the clouds
gather and the rain impends over the forest and our
house, permit us not to be cast down; let us not lose
the savour of past mercies and past pleasures; but,
like the voice of a bird singing in the rain, let grateful
memory survive in the hour of darkness. If there be
in front of us any painful duty, strengthen us with the
grace of courage; if any act of mercy, teach us
tenderness and patience.

ANOTHER IN TIME OF RAIN

Lord, Thou sendest down rain upon the uncounted
millions of the forest, and givest the trees to drink
exceedingly. We are here upon this isle a few
handfuls of men, and how many myriads upon
myriads of stalwart trees! Teach us the lesson of the
trees. The sea around us, which this rain recruits,
teems with the race of fish; teach us, Lord, the
meaning of the fishes. Let us see ourselves for what
we are, one out of the countless number of the clans
of thy handiwork. When we would despair, let us
remember that these also please and serve Thee.

FOR FRIENDS

For our absent loved ones we implore thy
loving-kindness. Keep them in life, keep them
in growing honour; and for us, grant that we
remain worthy of their love. For Christ's sake, let
not our beloved blush for us, nor we for them.
Grant us but that, and grant us courage to endure
lesser ills unshaken, and to accept death, loss, and
disappointment as it were straws upon the
tide of life.

BEFORE A TEMPORARY SEPARATION

To-day we go forth separate, some of us to
pleasure, some of us to worship, some upon duty.
Go with us, our guide and angel; hold Thou
before us in our divided paths the mark of our low
calling, still to be true to what small best we can
attain to. Help us in that, our maker, the dispenser
of events—Thou, of the vast designs, in which we
blindly labour, suffer us to be so far constant to
ourselves and our beloved.

FOR THE FAMILY

Aid us, if it be thy will, in our concerns. Have mercy on this land and innocent people. Help them who this day contend in disappointment with their frailties. Bless our family, bless our
forest house, bless our island helpers. Thou who hast made for us this place of ease and hope, accept and inflame our gratitude; help us to
repay, in service one to another, the debt of thine unmerited benefits and mercies, so that when the period of our stewardship draws to a conclusion, when the windows begin to be darkened, when the bond of the family is to be loosed, there shall be no bitterness of remorse in our farewells.

    Help us to look back on the long way that Thou hast brought us, on the long days in which we have been served not according to our deserts but our desires; on the pit and the miry clay, the blackness of despair, the horror of misconduct, from which our feet have been plucked out. For our sins forgiven or

prevented, for our shame unpublished, we bless
and thank Thee, O God. Help us yet again and ever.
So order events, so strengthen our frailty, as that day
by day we shall come before Thee with this song
of gratitude, and in the end we be dismissed with
honour. In their weakness and their fear, the
vessels of thy handiwork so pray to Thee,
so praise Thee. Amen.

FOR SELF-BLAME

Lord, enlighten us to see the beam that is in our
own eye, and blind us to the mote that is in
our brother's. Let us feel our offences with our
hands, make them great and bright before us like the
sun, make us eat them and drink them for our diet.
Blind us to the offences of our beloved, cleanse
them from our memories, take them out of our
mouths for ever. Let all here before Thee carry and
measure with the false balances of love, and be in
their own eyes and in all conjunctures the most
guilty. Help us at the same time with the grace of
courage, that we be none of us cast down when we
sit lamenting amid the ruins of our happiness or our
integrity: touch us with fire from the altar, that we
may be up and doing to rebuild our city: in the
name and by the method of him in whose words of
prayer we now conclude.

SUNDAY

We beseech Thee, Lord, to behold us with
favour, folk of many families and nations gathered
together in the peace of this roof, weak men and
women subsisting under the covert of thy patience.
Be patient still; suffer us yet awhile longer;—with our
broken purposes of good, with our idle endeavors
against evil, suffer us awhile longer to endure and
(if it may be) help us to do better. Bless to us our
extraordinary mercies; if the day come when these
must be taken, brace us to play the man under
affliction. Be with our friends, be with ourselves.
Go with each of us to rest; if any awake, temper to
them the dark hours of watching; and when the day
returns, return to us, our sun and comforter, and call
us up with morning faces and with morning hearts—
eager to labour—eager to be happy, if happiness
shall be our portion—and if the day be marked for
sorrow, strong to endure it.

   We thank Thee and praise Thee; and in the
words of him to whom this day is sacred,
close our oblation.

FOR SELF-FORGETFULNESS

Lord, the creatures of thy hand, thy disinherited
children, come before Thee with their incoherent
wishes and regrets: Children we are, children we
shall be, till our mother the earth hath fed upon our
bones. Accept us, correct us, guide us, thy guilty
innocents. Dry our vain tears, wipe out our vain
resentments, help our yet vainer efforts. If there be
any here, sulking as children will, deal with and
enlighten him. Make it day about that person, so that
he shall see himself and be ashamed. Make it heaven
about him, Lord, by the only way to heaven,
forgetfulness of self, and make it day about his
neighbours, so that they shall help, not hinder him.

FOR RENEWAL OF JOY

We are evil, O God, and help us to see it and
amend. We are good, and help us to be better.
Look down upon thy servants with a patient eye,
even as Thou sendest sun and rain; look down,
call upon the dry bones, quicken, enliven; recreate
in us the soul of service, the spirit of peace; renew
in us the sense of joy.

NOTE

In 1888 Robert Louis Stevenson, the celebrated author of *Kidnapped, Treasure Island, Dr. Jekyll & Mr. Hyde* and *A Child's Garden of Verses*, set sail with his family for the South Seas. After years of travel, they made their new home on a Samoan island with "beautiful rivers...pleasant fords and waterfalls and overhanging verdure." Stevenson lived his last few years there. They called their homestead "Vailima," after the five streams that flowed through it.

Stevenson thrived in this pioneer's tropical paradise, in a landscape physically demanding yet serenely beautiful, among cultures diverse and often divergent. Here Stevenson experimented with new means of expressing the richness of these experiences, among them the Prayers which he shared each evening with his family and Samoan household.

Scholars have questioned why Stevenson would embrace the ritual and form of prayer in his late life, in view of his known earlier criticism of religious orthodoxy. What is unquestioned is the resulting, exquisite use of liturgical literary tradition.

Stevenson's boundless love of nature is expressed with a humility and awe which we associate with the Old Testament, made more powerful by his conscious use of language from that early, formal yet familiar stylistic tradition. ("Lord, Thou sendest down rain upon the uncounted millions of the forest, and givest the trees to drink exceedingly. We are here upon this isle a few handfuls of men, and how many myriads upon myriads of stalwart trees! Teach us the lesson of the trees!")

Equally timeless are the thoughts expressed, often in direct, even modern language skillfully interwoven with traditional lyricism. ("The day returns and brings us the petty round of irritating concerns and duties. Help us to play the man, help us to perform them with laughter and kind faces, let cheerfulness abound with industry.")

And sonorous throughout the Prayers is Stevenson's enduring gratitude for the simple elements of our daily lives: for home, "for the health, the work, the food, and the bright skies, that make our lives delightful."

Distinctive to the Prayers is the dual character of Stevenson's petitions, appeals which are made as directly to us, his kindred, as to God. He asks that all of God's children be given "the grace to accept and forgive," to "blind us from the offences of our beloved," and to "let our loving-kindness make bright this house of our habitation." And he entreats us, the "folk of many families and nations," as well as God, to be patient with our imperfect efforts and to persevere.

Perhaps this is the greatest import of Stevenson's Prayers. Using a pure, simple and purposed form he urges us, with God's help, to look beyond ourselves, to be kind to each other, and, above all, to be grateful for the human struggle to live inspired.

PENELOPE GLASS

CALAMUS
Quality Gift & Trade Editions

Cataloging-in-Publication Data
Stevenson, Robert Louis, 1850-1894
      Prayers written at Vailima / by Robert Louis
      Stevenson; Catherine Kanner, artist; introduction
      by Mrs. R. L. Stevenson; Penelope Glass, editor.
      --1st ed.
      p. cm.
      LCCN: 00-103845
      ISBN: 0-9700689-0-5

      1. Prayers. I. Kanner, Catherine.
  II. Glass, Penelope. III. Title.

PR5488.P75 2000   828.8
                                  QBI00-500156

Printed in Hong Kong